Walking By Faith

Interactive Family Devotional

Rev. Dr. Denise Parker Lawrence

Archway Publishing books may be ordered through booksellers or by contacting:

Archway Publishing
1663 Liberty Drive
Bloomington, IN 47403
www.archwaypublishing.com
844-669-3957

ISBN: 978-1-6657-5442-2 (sc)
ISBN: 978-1-6657-5443-9 (e)

Library of Congress Control Number: 2023923858

Print information available on the last page.

Archway Publishing rev. date: 12/19/2023

Dear Family,

Train up a child in the way he *[she]* should go,

And even when he *[she]* is old *[she]* he will not depart from it.

[emphasis mine]

Proverbs 22:6

I relish the memories of my great-grandmother Elder Minnie Hudson, who imparted to me my initial love of the Lord. As I became a grandparent, I wanted to pass on her legacy. I wrote this book with themes and memory verses for the purpose of equipping and empowering you to "hide thy word" (Psalm 119:11 KJV) in the hearts and minds of the children entrusted in your care. I encourage you to read through the book, take a theme, and explore complementary verses in God's Word that will place these eternal treasures within your son, daughter, grandchild, niece, nephew, or any young person who calls you special. God's Word is truly the greatest gift you could ever provide. Explore ways to have fun through drawing, acting, and poetry writing as you share God's Word together. Enjoy!

Agape from a proud grandmother, Rev. Dr. Denise Parker Lawrence.

Please note all scriptures are taken from the American Standard or King James Version unless stated otherwise.

"Jesus Loves Me," Bradbury,1862. Setting: William B. Bradbury, 1866. Public Domain.

This book is dedicated to Alia, Ryan, Addison, Ava, Madison, William Isaiah, and Ji'Anna. You have been the fulfillment of God's promise that he would bless unto the second and third generation. Love, Big Grandma.

I extend a special shout-out to my baby girl, Maya Lawrence, who served as my muse, and to my granddaughter Addison, my in-house illustrator and writer.

Thank you to my loving and supportive family: Mort, Michcle, Yemi, Mac, and Camille.

FAITH

For we walk by faith, not by sight
(2 Corinthians 5:7).

"God leads me even when I cannot see with my eyes."

Discussion Point: How can we develop faith in the midst of challenges?

POWER

I can do all things through Christ which strengthens me (Philippians 4:13 KJV).

"I can do all things through Christ who makes me strong."

Discussion Point: How do I develop strength to tackle the things that I find difficult?

FEAR

For God hath not given us the spirit of fear; but of power, and of love, and of a sound mind (2 Timothy 1:7 KJV).

"I have power. God said I don't have to be afraid!"

Discussion Point: How do I overcome my fears?

ANGER

Be angry but do not sin; do not let the sun go down on your anger (Ephesians 4:26).

"As the sun sets, I will work on my anger before I do something bad just because I'm mad."

"I'm sorry, you take it first."

Exercise: Review a time when you have been angry, and talk about how you resolved it. Reflect by using journaling, art therapy, or a feeling wheel to process feelings.

SELF-CONTROL

But the fruit of the Spirit is love, joy and peace, patience, kindness, goodness, faithfulness, gentleness and self-control: against such there is no law (Galatians 5:22).

"I choose to make positive choices."

Discussion Question: How can I exercise self-control and make positive choices?

Positive Choices Tree

Peace

Gentleness

Joy

Patience

Goodness

Love

Self-Control

Negative Choices Tree

Bullying

Mean-spiritedness

Anger

Unfriendly

Mad

The little girl looks at both trees and says, "I make positive choices".

PEACE

And the peace of God, which passeth all understanding, shall keep your hearts and minds through Christ Jesus (Philippians 4:7 KJV).

"Even if I'm not sure of what's going on and feel nervous, God will be with me and give me peace within."

Discussion Question: What makes you feel peaceful?

WISDOM

The fear of the Lord is the beginning of wisdom (Proverbs 9:10 KJV).

"I read to be smart, but I'm wise because I listen to God and obey God's commandments in my heart."

Exercise: Have your child talk about a challenge he or she has had. Have them write a chart of positive choices and negative choices. What made them choose the positive choice?

TRUST

Trust in the Lord with all your heart and lean not to your own understanding (Proverb 3:5 KJV).

Children: "Lord, we trust that you will take care of our friend, although he looks very sick."

Discussion Point: How do I know the difference between God's voice and those of others?

PURPOSE

I know the plans I have for you, declares the LORD. Plans to prosper you and not to harm you, plans to give you hope and a future (Jeremiah 29:11 KJV).

- -

Child: "I want to be a chef, lawyer, illustrator, scientist, actor or _____."

- -

Exercise: Draw or create a goal sheet; incorporate long-term and short-term goals.

RESPECT

Honor your father and mother … which is the first commandment with a promise (Ephesians 6:2).

"I'm happy to listen to my parents because it makes God proud of me."

Exercise: Discuss benefits of children being respectful intergenerationally to adults, teachers, police officers, and community leaders.

JOY

The joy of the Lord is my strength (Nehemiah 8:10).

"I become stronger when I focus on what makes God happy, and that brings me joy. I don't let others steal my joy."

Exercise: Encourage your child to draw a picture, make a collage, or write a poem about joy.

"I'm joyful in spite of others"

LOVE

For God so loved the world, that he gave his only begotten Son, that whosoever believeth on him should not perish, but have eternal life. (John 3:16 ASV).

"God loved us so much that he gave us Jesus. His love will never leave us."

We are grateful, so we sing: "Yes, Jesus loves me; yes, Jesus loves me; yes, Jesus loves me because the Bible tells me so!"

Discussion point: What does it mean to have sacrificial love?

"Yes, Jesus loves me;
Jesus loves me;
yes, Jesus loves me
because the Bible tells me so!"

Feeling Wheel

How are you feeling today?

Let's talk about it!

FEELING WHEEL

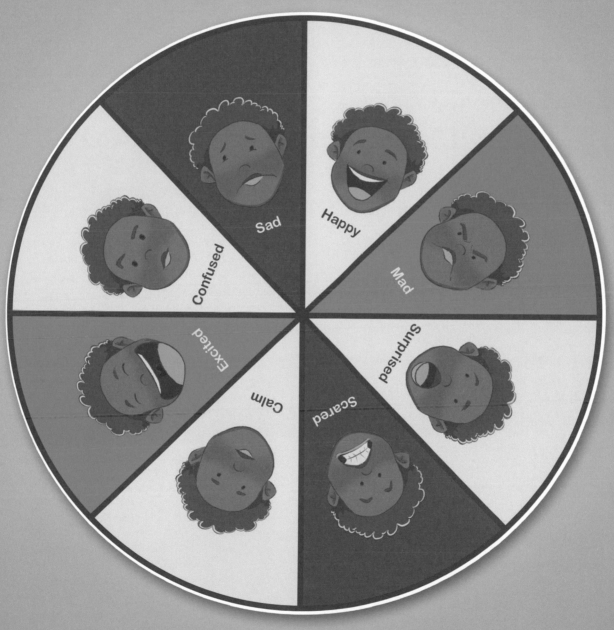

Hide Thy Word in Their Hearts

Table Blessings: "God is good, God is great, and we thank him for our food. Amen."

Bedtime Prayer: "Now I lay me down to sleep; I pray The Lord my soul to keep. If I should die before I wake, I pray the Lord my soul to take."

Psalm 23(KJV)

The LORD is my shepherd; I shall not want.

He maketh me to lie down in green pastures:
he leadeth me beside the still waters.

He restoreth my soul: he leadeth me in the paths
of righteousness for his name's sake.

Yea, though I walk through the valley of the shadow
of death, I will fear no evil: for thou art with me;
thy rod and thy staff they comfort me.

Thou preparest a table before me in the presence of mine enemies:
thou anointest my head with oil; my cup runneth over.

Surely goodness and mercy shall follow me all the days of my
life: and I will dwell in the house of the LORD for ever.

The Lord's Prayer
Matthew 6:9–12 (KJV)

Our Father which art in heaven, Hallowed be thy name.

Thy kingdom come, Thy will be done in earth, as it is in heaven.

Give us this day our daily bread.
And forgive us our debts, as we forgive our debtors.

And lead us not into temptation, but deliver us from evil: For thine
is the kingdom, and the power, and the glory, for ever. Amen.

Printed in the United States
by Baker & Taylor Publisher Services